Date: 2/28/20

Wild Weather
Hurricanes

by Julie Murray

Dash!
LEVELED READERS
3

³ **Dash!**
LEVELED READERS

Level 1 – Beginning
Short and simple sentences with familiar words or patterns for children who are beginning to understand how letters and sounds go together.

Level 2 – Emerging
Longer words and sentences with more complex language patterns for readers who are practicing common words and letter sounds.

Level 3 – Transitional
More developed language and vocabulary for readers who are becoming more independent.

abdopublishing.com
Published by Abdo Zoom, a division of ABDO, P.O. Box 398166, Minneapolis, Minnesota 55439.
Copyright © 2018 by Abdo Consulting Group, Inc. International copyrights reserved in all countries.
No part of this book may be reproduced in any form without written permission from the publisher.

Printed in the United States of America, North Mankato, Minnesota.
092017
012018

Photo Credits: iStock, Shutterstock
Production Contributors: Kenny Abdo, Jennie Forsberg, Grace Hansen, John Hansen
Design Contributors: Dorothy Toth

Publisher's Cataloging in Publication Data
Names: Murray, Julie, author.
Title: Hurricanes / by Julie Murray.
Description: Minneapolis, Minnesota: Abdo Zoom, 2018. | Series: Wild weather |
    Includes online resource and index.
Identifiers: LCCN 2017939263 | ISBN 9781532120886 (lib.bdg.) | ISBN 9781532122002 (ebook) |
    ISBN 9781532122569 (Read-to-Me ebook)
Subjects: LCSH: Hurricanes--Juvenile literature. | Weather--Juvenile literature. | Environment--Juvenile
    literature.
Classification: DDC 551.552--dc23
LC record available at https://lccn.loc.gov/2017939263

THIS BOOK CONTAINS
RECYCLED MATERIALS

Table of Contents

Hurricanes 4

How They Form 8

Parts of a Hurricane 12

More Facts 22

Glossary 23

Index 24

Online Resources 24

Hurricanes

Hurricanes are dangerous storms. They can cause great **damage**. Hurricane season in the U.S. is from June through November. On average, the U.S. is hit with two hurricanes each year.

Hurricanes are giant, spinning storms and can be 300 miles (482 km) wide! They form and travel over warm ocean waters. To be a hurricane, a storm must have wind speeds of at least 74 mph (119 kph).

How They Form

Hurricanes start as thunderstorms. The warm ocean water feeds the storm and it grows stronger, becoming a **tropical depression**.

If it keeps growing, it becomes a tropical storm. Some of these storms grow into hurricanes, others die out.

Hurricanes can be **devastating**. They can last for hours or sometimes even days.

They can cause flooding from heavy rain and **storm surge**. High winds can knockout power, and can level trees and homes.

Parts of a Hurricane

There are three main parts of a hurricane: the eye, the eye wall, and the rain bands. The eye of the storm is in the center. The storm rotates around this area. In the eye, the winds are calm and the skies are clear.

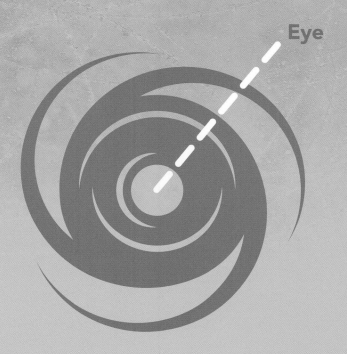

Eye

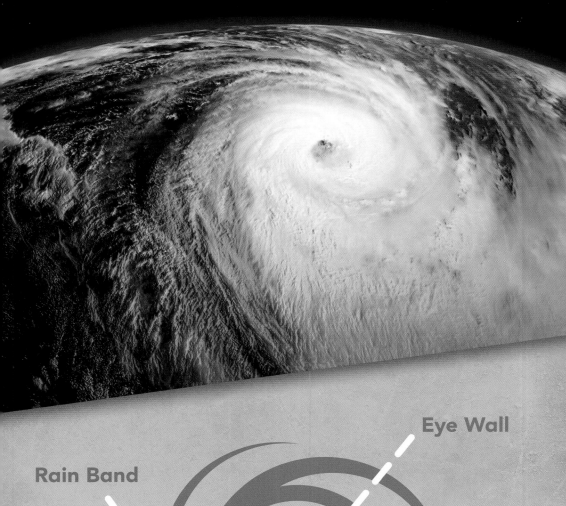

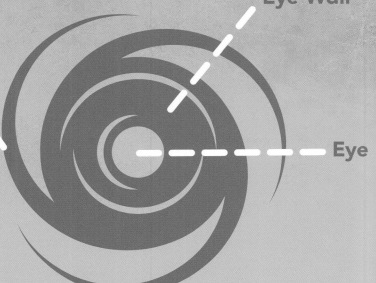

Rain Band

Eye Wall

Eye

The eye wall is the area that surrounds the eye. It is the strongest part of the storm. This is where the highest winds and heaviest rain occur. The rain bands spin around the eye wall. These bands give hurricanes their pinwheel look.

There are different categories of hurricanes. A category 1 storm is the weakest.

A category 5 storm is the strongest. Hurricane Katrina hit the U.S. in 2005. It was a category 5 storm with winds up to 175 mph (281 kph).

Meteorologists use satellites and radars to track storms. They can warn people if a hurricane is heading their way.

st Aid Kit

UPPLIES
Y SIGNA

Being prepared for a hurricane is important. Be sure to stock up on food and water.

Some people put boards on their windows. This protects them from high winds and flying **debris**.

More Facts

- Hurricanes that are north of the equator spin counterclockwise. If they are south of the equator, they spin clockwise.

- Hurricanes are named in alphabetical order. Each year they start with the letter A and rotate between boy and girl names.

- Ocean surface water must be at least 82 degrees F (27 degrees C) for a hurricane to form.

Glossary

damage – harm that makes something less useful or valuable.

debris – scattered pieces left after something has been destroyed.

devastating – highly destructive or damaging.

tropical depression – a cyclone in the tropics in which the maximum wind speed is 38 mph (62 kph) or less.

meteorologist – a weather forecaster.

storm surge – a rising of the sea as a result of atmospheric pressure and wind associated with a storm.

Index

categories 16, 17

damage 4, 11

danger 4

duration 10

eye 13, 14, 15

flooding 11

formation 6, 9

Hurricane Katrina 17

meteorologist 18

parts 13, 14, 15

preparation 20, 21

safety 20, 21

season 4

United States 4, 17

wind 6, 11

Online Resources

Booklinks
NONFICTION NETWORK
FREE! ONLINE NONFICTION RESOURCES

To learn more about hurricanes, please visit **abdobooklinks.com**. These links are routinely monitored and updated to provide the most current information available.